POSTMODERN ENCOUNTERS

Chomsky and Globalisation

Jeremy Fox

Series editor: Richard Appignanesi

ICON BOOKS UK

TOTEM BOOKS USA

Published in the UK in 2001
by Icon Books Ltd., Grange Road,
Duxford, Cambridge CB2 4QF
E-mail: info@iconbooks.co.uk
www.iconbooks.co.uk

Published in the USA in 2001
by Totem Books
Inquiries to: Icon Books Ltd.,
Grange Road, Duxford,
Cambridge CB2 4QF, UK

Sold in the UK, Europe, South Africa
and Asia by Faber and Faber Ltd.,
3 Queen Square, London WC1N 3AU
or their agents

Distributed to the trade in the USA by
National Book Network Inc.,
4720 Boston Way, Lanham,
Maryland 20706

Distributed in the UK, Europe,
South Africa and Asia by
Macmillan Distribution Ltd.,
Houndmills, Basingstoke RG21 6XS

Distributed in Canada by
Penguin Books Canada,
10 Alcorn Avenue, Suite 300,
Toronto, Ontario M4V 3B2

Published in Australia in 2001
by Allen & Unwin Pty. Ltd.,
83 Alexander Street,
Crows Nest, NSW 2065

Reprinted 2001, 2002

Text copyright © 2001 Jeremy Fox

The author has asserted his moral rights.

Series editor: Richard Appignanesi

ISBN 1 84046 237 X

Typesetting by Wayzgoose

Printed and bound in the UK by
Cox & Wyman Ltd., Reading

Introduction

Noam Chomsky is well placed to represent a left-wing view of globalisation and the new world order. He is well known, a prolific writer of books, articles and letters, and makes many speeches, so information about his views is easy to find. In his research work, he is known as the 'Einstein of modern linguistics', and almost universally admired by his colleagues for his contribution to their work. But as a commentator on political and social affairs, he arouses mixed feelings. Many socialists admire him warmly and would agree with much of what he says and writes. But some middle-of-the-road Americans find it hard to accept the unremitting severity of his attacks on American government policy, especially foreign policy. The irritation felt by some is expressed in this quotation from the prestigious *New York Times*:

Arguably the most important intellectual alive, how can he write such nonsense about international affairs and foreign policy?[1]

Another, similar viewpoint is expressed by a reader of the *Los Angeles Times* who wrote in 1988 that:

Noam Chomsky is a voice in the wilderness, but nobody listens.[2]

It is not particularly surprising if many in a society are patriotic and criticise those who attack government policy. After all, Darwin himself wrote on patriotism:

There can be no doubt that a tribe including many members who, from possessing in a high degree the spirit of patriotism, fidelity, obedience, courage and sympathy, were always ready to give aid to each other and to sacrifice themselves for the common good, would be victorious over most other tribes; and this would be natural selection.[3]

From our point of view, however, the qualities that are most useful in a commentator on globalisation are more likely to include readability, expertise and common sense than unquestioning acceptance of US government policy.

For over 30 years, Chomsky has been denouncing US foreign policy, complaining noisily about the way the USA has treated so many Third World countries. To take a typical example, he lectured at the American University in Cairo in 1993 about the Cold War period, during which US operations included 'the overthrow of the conservative parliamentary regime in Iran in 1953, restoring the Shah and his brutal rule; the destruction of Guatemala's ten year democratic interlude', which placed in power 'a collection of mass murderers who would have won nods of approval from Himmler and Goering', with atrocities reaching their highest level in the 1980s, 'always with the backing or participation of the United States and its client states'; and 'the establishment of a Latin-American style terror state in South Vietnam' . . . [4]

Chomsky is not alone in such attacks on US foreign policy. For example, Garry Wills noted the American tendency to dethrone elected leaders in Africa, Asia and Latin America, and substitute others that they have felt to be more suitable:

Over time, American leadership substituted for that of Muhammad Mossadeq in Iran, Jacobo Arbenz Guzmán in Guatemala, Patrice Lumumba in the Congo, Ngo Dinh Diem in South Vietnam, Rafael Trujillo in The Dominican Republic, Salvador Allende in Chile, Daniel Ortega in Nicaragua, Maurice Bishop in Grenada, and Manuel Noriega in Panama.[5]

The idea of the US as a 'bully' was reflected in the leading article in a British newspaper in March 1999. Referring to a trade dispute with the European Community about Caribbean bananas, *The Independent* newspaper recommended resisting the retaliatory tariffs imposed by the US on cashmere pullovers and possibly Concorde landing rights, commenting:

The behaviour of the United States is bullying, unconvincing, and illegal, and quite extraordinary for a nation which espouses the values of free trade and the rule of law.[6]

In actual fact, as Chomsky often makes clear,

America does not believe in free trade for itself at all, but only for non-Western countries. Free trade is imposed on the poor countries by the leaders of the world, whose industries and commerce have long been amply protected.

On matters of foreign policy, Chomsky often refers to the high level of indoctrination in his country, which makes most people – particularly in the educated classes – accept the government line. The reason for this, he explains, is that the educated classes are subjected to a constant flow of propaganda. It is largely directed at them because they are more important, so they have to be more closely controlled. Furthermore, 'the educated classes become the instruments of propaganda. Their function in the society is to promulgate and develop the ideological principles. As a result they inculcate them, if they don't they're usually weeded out and are no longer part of the privileged élite.'[7]

So the level of indoctrination among the American intelligentsia may be part of the explanation of the gap between Chomsky's views and the more politically correct and conventional views of American foreign policy.

Chomsky is a dissident, but a scholarly one. An example is his work on global politics, *World Orders, Old and New*. This book of 342 pages contains something like 850 references to other books, articles, newspapers etc. Furthermore, if a mistake ever does slip into any of his publications, he makes sure it is corrected in later versions. Thus James McGilvray writes:

[H]*e constantly updates his discussion of issues and areas; his work on Israel is an example.*[8]

The work on the Middle East to which McGilvray is referring includes the original edition of Chomsky's *Fateful Triangle – The United States, Israel and The Palestinians*. This first came out in 1983, but was republished in an updated edition in 1999. (The later edition included 92 extra pages, plus notes, in three new chapters.) And of course Chomsky is well aware that, if his work were ever slipshod, he would soon be exposed by his detractors. In fact, he seems to see himself as a sort of guardian of truth and provider of accurate information. Indeed, Chomsky has specifically written:

What I'm trying to do is simply provide the service to popular dissident movements and scattered individuals that any person who has the resources, the privilege, the training, etc. should perform, nothing beyond that.[9]

Some may be tempted to idolise Chomsky, who is clearly a remarkable person. There is a nice vignette by Norman Mailer, dating back to 1967:

Later in the year, his cell mate during one night in jail, Norman Mailer, who had heard that Chomsky, 'though barely thirty, was considered a genius at MIT for his new contribution to linguistics', would portray him as 'a slim sharp-featured man with an ascetic expression, and an air of gentle but absolute moral integrity'.[10]

And Carlos Otero, editor of Chomsky's *Language and Politics*, speaks of him in relation to the prophetic traditions of both the Enlightenment and recent Jewish writings.[11] On a more everyday level, he is known to be kind to those who ask him for help, and normally answers inquiries with a minimum of delay, often within a few hours.

It seems likely that Jewish tradition influenced Chomsky when he was young. Otero mentions a study which describes the special contribution of Jewish immigrants to American life during the period 1880–1920 (the period during which Chomsky's parents came over from Russia):

Socialism for them was more than a social doctrine; it was an ethical system which, when taken seriously, as many libertarians do, leads to building a thoroughly new society.[12]

The Jewish tradition and Enlightenment influences probably had an impact on Chomsky's thinking, such as the belief that the goal of cultural change in the broadest sense (including revolutionary social change) is the pursuit of justice, not the conquest of power.[13]

Whether he is writing about linguistics or commenting on global economics or American attacks on the Third World, his views are simply expressed, yet often startlingly original. He claims that:

I'm really not interested in persuading people, I don't want to and I try to make this point obvious. What I'd like to do is to help people persuade themselves.[14]

Politics and Linguistics

Interviewers of Chomsky have sometimes asked him if there is a link between his political and humanitarian work and his work in linguistics. There are some links of a personal nature: some of his political friends when he was a young man were also interested in linguistics. Chomsky's interest in politics dates from an early age. He used to meet with other East-European emigrés and intellectuals from the Jewish working class. They met at his uncle's kiosk in New York, and sometimes talked all night. Linguistics was part of his life from childhood onwards: his father was a 'noted Hebrew scholar',[15] and Chomsky himself later wrote a grammar of Hebrew as a thesis while he was an undergraduate at the University of Pennsylvania.[16] His supervisor there, Zellig Harris, was a libertarian anarchist. In fact,

Chomsky first met Harris in connection with political work before they collaborated in linguistics. (The political matter was about plans for Chomsky to live on a kibbutz, and work for cooperation between Arabs and Jews.)[17]

Otero quotes a tentative statement by Chomsky in 1981 on whether there is a possible relationship between his linguistics and his politics:

I believe that the study of human cognitive structure and human intellectual achievement reveals a high degree of genetically determined innate structure that lies at the basis of the creative aspect of human intellectual achievement, which is easily perceived in every aspect of normal intellectual achievement, most strikingly, most easily, perhaps, in the acquisition and free use of the system of language, which permit the free expression of thought over an unbounded range.[18]

Chomsky goes on to speculate about there being an instinct for freedom, but notes that there was not, at that time, enough evidence to establish this. This makes him extremely cautious about drawing any connections between these areas.

Later, in 1988, Chomsky was asked by his editor, Carlos Otero:

There is the Chomsky who is a scientist and linguist and the Chomsky who engages in political struggles. What do they say to each other when they meet?

Chomsky replied carefully:

There is no connection, apart from some very tenuous relations at an abstract level, for example, with regard to a concept of human freedom that animates both endeavors.[19]

However, a new book about Chomsky suggests that his political and linguistic works seem to be part of a 'unified project'. This might be a philosophical project which puts his work within a coherent research paradigm that dates back to Descartes and involves a certain view of human nature. This view *may* suggest a link between Chomsky's work as a linguist and his work as a political analyst and advocate. McGilvray's book develops the theme.[20]

In December 1984, Chomsky said that he would assume, or at least hope, that there was 'some sort of, what Bakunin once called an "instinct for freedom"', in other words, 'a commitment to be free of the constraints of external authority' except insofar as they were 'required for survival in that particular stage of history'.[21]

Thus, there may be a link between the 'creative aspect of language use' and Chomsky's libertarian political activities, perhaps in the sense of their both being focussed on freedom and creativity. Furthermore, just as Chomsky is careful not to make unwarranted claims about possible links between his politics and his linguistics, he objects on principle to unjustified claims of authority over human beings. For Chomsky, the defence of freedom involves challenging illegitimate claims to authority and power. As he once put it, in the *Anderson Valley Advertiser*, '[a]ny form of authority requires justification'. That is to say, 'it's not self-justified. And the justification can rarely be given.' Occasionally one can give it: he accepted that there is a valid argument that one should not let a three-year-old run across the street. That would be a form of justifiable authority.

But there aren't many of them, and usually the effort to give a justification fails. And when we try to face it, we find that the authority is illegitimate. And any time you find a form of authority illegitimate, you ought to challenge it.[22]

The 'tenuous relation' between language and politics in his life may also relate to Chomsky's view that human beings may have an innate biological endowment to develop moral systems – a 'mental organ of moral evaluation', perhaps comparable to the innate component to develop creative language use on which he worked early in his research. Chomsky has also drawn attention to the work of Wilhelm von Humboldt (1767–1835):

Humboldt was, on the one hand, one of the most profound theorists of general linguistics, and on the other, an early and forceful advocate of libertarian values.[23]

Chomsky as Dissident

Some have dismissed Chomsky's unconventional views, or refused to take him seriously. It is clear that, for 40 years and more, he has been attacking the policies of the American government:

- For frequent assaults on Third World countries, particularly in Latin America and the Far East;[24]
- For reducing the standards of living and health-care for many of its own citizens, and those in other countries;[25]
- For allowing children to exist in serious poverty in cities like New York.[26]

Chomsky is also a dissident in opposing:

- The authoritarian, tyrannical and anti-democratic structures of the TNCs (trans-national corporations, also known as 'multi-nationals');[27]
- The many gaps between the US government's claims and its actual deeds;
- The growth in inequality within both rich and poor countries.[28]

Finally, he is an unusual person:

- In his concern for complete accuracy, and for the avoidance of exaggerated or unfounded claims;[29]
- In his personal courage in submitting himself to hostility and personal abuse at public meetings;[30]
- In his willingness to answer e-mails and help others attain their aims, whether they are young students of linguistics, anarchist groups, or odd people writing books.

The Arrival of Globalisation

Chomsky is a persuasive arguer, a persistent critic of government policy and the activities of the huge (mainly American) TNCs. However, now that we have entered the third millennium, many would agree that globalisation is securely established, and indeed probably generally felt by the majority to be something positive which is leading the world to a richer, happier future.

Since Chomsky is an unusual person, sceptical about many conventional beliefs, it seems best to look next at some widespread views on globalisation and problems associated with it, and only then to look further at Chomsky's views in particular. Chomsky is a prolific writer, and has written over 75 books since 1957 (most of his publications before then were about linguistics). But globalisation is a recent phenomenon. So, in order to concentrate on recent developments, most quotes have been taken from Chomsky's books, talks and interviews published since 1994.

Globalisation first appeared towards the end of the 20th century. It was a time when, for the Marxist historian Eric Hobsbawm, the world had reached a critical stage. In the late 1980s and early 90s, an era of world history ended and a new one began.[31] The Soviet Union collapsed and much of its wealth was absorbed by Western business interests. Information Technology, or 'IT' for short, was continuing its headlong development, linking the world together electronically in global networks of computers and communications devices, making international trade and speculation faster and easier to carry out. Air freight of food boomed, and all year through, fresh fruit and vegetables from all over the world filled the supermarkets of the West. Personal computers became cheaper and more powerful. Mobile phones took off. And excited talk of 'globalisation' and 'innovation' spread like wildfire, as many saw in globalisation better ways of becoming rich.

But why is it called *globalisation*? The 'global' part of 'globalisation' contrasts with 'local', as in 'local government'. Globalisation has been described as the shift from local to global control:

The process whereby state-centric agencies and terms of reference are dissolved in a structure of relations between different actors operating in a context which is truly global rather than merely international.[32]

Worldwide links are emphasised in a description of globalisation by David Held (et al.) as:

[A] *process (or set of processes) which embodies a transformation in the spatial organisation of social relations and transactions – assessed in terms of their extensity, intensity, velocity and impact – generating transcontinental or inter-regional flows and networks of activity.*[33]

The 'Global Market' and the end of Nation States

Supporters of globalisation are said to wish to turn the world into one big global market.[34] As a result, globalisation seems to be weakening the power of individual countries to control their own destinies, and major decisions are increasingly made higher up, at a global level. The influence of national governments is reduced. In fact, several advanced countries in the OECD (Organisation for Economic Cooperation and Development – mainly Western European countries, plus Canada, Japan and the USA), including Britain, have handed responsibility for determining national interest rates over to their Central Banks, thereby abandoning national capital controls and eliminating the formal barriers between domestic and international markets.[35] According to Hobsbawm, the German sociologist Ulrich Beck has spoken of the 'jubilant mass suicide' of politicians as they jump on the bandwagon and sing the praises of the market, thus undermining their own position in the process.[36]

Businesses now have to compete globally. The claimed existence of this 'global market', in which everyone competes with everyone else, might be little more than a trick. For example, if the argument about 'competition in the global economy' is exaggerated, the claim may be a device to reduce production costs by keeping the workforce insecure and easier to control. Thus the 'New Work Order' is believed by some to be primarily concerned with cutting costs, raising salaries and bonuses of top management, and maximising profits for owners and investors.[37] None of these, it goes without saying, is related to the needs of the workforce.

The question of 'The Control of Truth by the Corporate' is a major theme of Chomsky's. The problem of this control has not gone away with globalisation – probably the reverse. Indeed, the power and sophistication of the media provide ever more powerful ways of influencing how people think, and what they believe.

For some time, Chomsky has been drawing attention to the way in which Big Business distorts our perception of the truth. This distortion and confusion goes back a century or more, and is a threat to our freedom. Chomsky describes this practice as 'the growth of corporate propaganda to undermine democracy'. For example, he remarks that the US has a public relations industry which was established 'approximately at the same time that corporations reached their current form early in the [20th] century'. Its purpose was 'to control the public mind, because [industrialists] recognized that the public mind would be the greatest hazard facing [them], and understood that democracy is a real threat to private tyranny, just as it's a threat to state tyranny'.[38]

For Chomsky, the fact that democracy is a threat to private business helps to explain 'the extraordinary scale of the efforts "to indoctrinate people with the capitalist story"'.[39]

It also suggests that in certain aspects of economic globalisation, things have not changed much; in particular, the aims of bosses and workers. The impact of globalisation up to now has been to raise profits, strengthen the corporate, and weaken the workforce. But in the new capitalist global order it is the super-rich élite groups, most of them investors in Third World countries, which are the real beneficiaries. The system has not changed. Rather, it has become more extreme through the growth of inequality.

Globalisation and Capitalism

Economic globalisation can be seen as the latest version of capitalism. One could say that capitalism has taken over the opportunities (e.g. communications, speed and efficiency) that globalisation has given it, and become stronger and more efficient in the process. Historians trace capitalism back several centuries. Díaz Arenas, for example, follows it back to the mercantile capitalism of the 15th century in the days when Spain and Portugal ruled the waves.[40] So, from this viewpoint, we can see globalisation as continuing a long historical tradition. But what are the essential features of capitalism?

Will Hutton and Anthony Giddens identify three basic characteristics of capitalism:

- First, it is a system of the private ownership of property;
- Second, economic activity is guided by price signals set in markets;
- And third, it expects and depends upon the motivation for action to be the quest for profit.[41]

From his standpoint as a libertarian socialist who saw the distress of the American urban unemployed in his childhood, Chomsky has long been opposed to 'predatory capitalism'. As early as 1973, he wrote that it was 'not a fit system' for the mid-20th century. It was 'incapable of meeting human needs that can be expressed only in collective terms', and its concept of competitive man who 'seeks only to maximise wealth and power, who subjects himself to market relationships, to exploitation and external authority, [was] antihuman and intolerable in the deepest sense'.[42]

According to neo-liberal theory, for capitalism

to operate best, state intervention (e.g. through taxes and controls) has to be excluded. Markets should be deregulated, 'set free' and left to find their own level. Taxes and all forms of government control are an intrusion on free trade.

Furthermore, with the demise of the Soviet Union, the world financial system has virtually fallen into the hands of 'global capitalism'. So far, we have been talking of economic globalisation. But there are other types of globalisation in addition to the economic. Globalisation occurs in the media, at a cultural level, in politics, war, finance, migration and the environment.[43]

Ironically, of all the different forms of global capitalism, international crime looks set to be:

[A] *defining issue of the 21st century as the cold war was for the 20th century and colonialism was for the 19th century. Transnational crime will proliferate because crime groups are the major beneficiaries of globalisation. For example, crime on the Internet is presenting police forces with a growing challenge.*[44]

For some time, drug-trafficking has been a major area of operation for global crime; but the slow disappearance of work, the growth of inequality, and the impoverishment of the Third World are leading to a growth of refugee trafficking (e.g. from China to the UK). As Europe's population continues to drop, and that of the Third World continues to grow, and with many of them without work, the number of would-be illegal immigrants seems bound to go on growing. Sadly, the collapse of Third World industries and loss of Third World jobs are largely caused by the operations of global capitalism, including globalisation.[45]

Features of Globalisation

1. Three Views

David Held and his colleagues divide the different positions in the debate about globalisation into three main groups:

- Hyperglobalisers believe that globalisation is growing fast and affecting us all more and more, so that our lives are all subject to the disciplines of the global market.[46]

- Sceptics like Paul Hirst and Graham Thompson tend to the view that several of the claims about globalisation have been exaggerated. In fact, world trade is made up of three main blocks: Europe, Asia-Pacific and North America. There existed no model, they wrote in 1996, of what the global economy was actually like. In fact, many of the arguments of the radical globalists (i.e. hyperglobalisers) were shallow and unfounded.[47]

- Transformationalists like Giddens see globalisation in wider terms than global economics alone. For them:

[G]*lobalization is a central driving force behind the rapid social, political and economic changes that are reshaping modern societies and world order.*[48]

2. Aim

The basic aim of economic globalisation is to globalise the entire world economy, and since the

US is by far the richest country and controls the world economy (with the support of its allies and the mainly unelected agencies like the International Monetary Fund, World Bank and World Trade Organisation), this means, in effect, that the world economy is being adapted inexorably to suit US investors and the US economy. This process is now in full swing. As Will Hutton commented drily in conversation with Anthony Giddens:

My point [. . .] is that liberal America has its back against the wall; that the conservatives are in the ascendant; and that they have been ruthless in pursuit of their interests, compromising the American Presidency and shaping globalisation in US interests.[49]

3. Lean and Mean

Hutton and Giddens also point out that global capitalism is now getting tougher and more cut-throat. It's like a game: if you win, you do very well; otherwise, 'Tough, baby!'. In a globalised world, it is somehow seen as right and proper that the winners should end up enormously rich, while the losers end up on the breadline. Since the global economic system is based on profit, inequality is normal, natural and desirable.[50]

4. Impact of IT

The use of IT doesn't just aid business communications. It works so fast, bouncing messages across the world and back, that if figures increase by 0.1 per cent each time, these small differences can be magnified many times in speculative activity.

Small amounts of actual capital can be leveraged to create large deals with many interlocking variables, each affecting the rest. These transactions are of such intricacy that in many cases they are not fully understood by the companies that promote them.[51]

70 per cent of global economic activity is speculation, and in 'the windowless bunkers in which fortunes are made, nothing is produced'.[52] Nothing, that is, except wealth.

5. Winners and Losers

In a system whose main purpose is profit, one may ask, *For whom?* The established wisdom, as seen in the press and on TV worldwide, is that, under globalisation and free trade, all will benefit. Robert Beynon sees free trade as the way to prosperity:

Free trade is not only desirable, it is the biggest single impetus for global prosperity.[53]

President Clinton's vision is that globalisation will lead to freedom, democracy and peace:

[G]lobalisation is about more than economics. Our purpose must be to bring together the world around freedom, democracy and peace, and to oppose those who would tear it apart. Here are the fundamental challenges I believe America must meet to shape the 21st century.[54]

A common argument in favour of unregulated free trade is that it will lead to a general rise in living standards. Experience has shown that, with the opening up of trade and financial markets, investors, entrepreneurs and professionals have made a lot of money; but many of the poorest countries have been victims of a marked drop in living standards.[55]

Although it does seem a little hard to believe that everyone is going to win out in a competitive free market system, claims to this effect are sometimes made. For example, no less than the head of the World Trade Organisation, the New Zealander Mike Moore, reported in June 2000 on some research that had been conducted by academics at the Universities of Tel Aviv and Sussex:

[T]*he more open an economy to trade, the faster it can catch up with the developed countries. And poor people within developing countries tend to benefit most from trade liberalisation.*[56]

The point here is not to refute this piece of research. Rather, it is that Moore's report is an example of the way in which the World Trade Organisation is trying to defend free trade, which is becoming necessary as attacks on it spread, whether from the left, as at the December 1999 Seattle meeting of the World Trade Organisation, or by the Churches lobbying the 'Great Powers' at meetings of G-8 (the Group of Eight Great Powers: USA, Germany, Japan, France, UK, Canada, Italy and, recently, Russia). In much the same way, the International Monetary Fund (IMF) publishes many 'academic studies' about the success of its operations, out-numbering alternative studies on the IMF. (Propaganda, like advertising, requires sustained effort.) But in fact, the Third World has suffered considerably under globalised free trade, and it is possible that the word is beginning to get around.

6. Globalisation Has Not Reversed 25 Years of Decline

- Under globalisation, most of the profits go to the élite groups, to American investors and American TNCs (transnational corporations).
- For Third World countries, involvement in globalisation, in particular through free trade and the rescheduling of debts, has been disastrous, as will be seen.

- For the world in general, globalisation has yet to bring higher standards of living. Indications so far are that it will not do so. Global capitalism is generally oriented towards short-term profits which benefit the few, rather than towards long-term social benefits for the many. In the way it currently operates, global capitalism is more focussed on the desires of privileged individuals than on benefit for the community as a whole.

Indeed, Chomsky even points out that global economic growth has dropped, not risen, over the last 25 years. (The term 'globalisation' has been in use for about the last ten years of this period.) He writes that:

[F]or the majority of the population even in the superrich US, wages have stagnated or declined since 25 years ago while working hours and insecurity have greatly increased, [. . .] global economic growth has declined in the same period (quite considerably), [. . .] for a huge part of the

33

world's population conditions are awful and often deteriorating, and most importantly [. . .] the correlation between economic growth and social welfare that has often held (e.g. during the post-war period, pre-liberalization) has been severed.[57]

Even in the USA, leader of the Free World, 20 per cent of the population were living in a state of *postmodern poverty* in 1998, when William Finnegan's book *Cold New World* was published:

While the national economy has been growing, the economic prospects of most Americans have been dimming. For young people and males and those without advanced degrees – for, that is, the vast majority of working Americans, real hourly wages have fallen significantly over the past twenty-four years. [. . .] What the triumphalism of most American business writing ignores is a frightening growth in low-wage jobs. This growth has left 30 per cent of the country as workers earning too little to lift a family out of poverty.[58]

To summarise, globalisation has not yet reversed the pattern of 25 years of poverty for 30 per cent of Americans. Nor is it improving conditions for the bulk of the population, even in rich Western countries. Furthermore, it is unlikely to bring any such improvements. What is more likely is that more and more of the profits and natural resources are being sucked away to sustain the 'élite groups', keep them in comfort, and protect them against attack. Increasing attacks on the super-rich seem likely at some stage. Housing for the very rich in America is now often surrounded by high walls, with only a single guarded entrance. Maybe wars in the future will occur between the rich and poor of each country, as well as between unemployed aspiring illegal immigrants from the South trying to break in to find work in an increasingly barricaded North. Meanwhile, the media portray would-be immigrants as a threat to the national standard of living, and racism grows.

7. Inequality

Whatever dreams people may have about progress, and about building a better world, economic globalisation seems bound to continue to
produce a growing gap between rich and poor in
the prosperous West, and an even vaster gap
between rich and poor countries in the world as a
whole. Hobsbawm summarises the position:

*[W]e cannot overlook the extraordinary increase
of the global gap between the rich and the poor
in the era of free-market fundamentalism.* [. . .]
*Patently, a billion people living in dire poverty
alongside a billion in widening splendour in a
planet growing ever smaller and more integrated
is not a sustainable scenario.*[59]

Statistics like these do serve to make one thing
clear. They tell us why those who do so well out
of globalisation are so keen to extol its virtues to
those who don't.

A case of 'what's good for me is obviously good
for you as well'.

Neo-liberalism, as the term is now generally re-deployed (particularly in global circles), sadly, refers to rather different views and values, making competitive self-seeking and the quest for profit the queen of the virtues. Neo-liberalism presents itself as the latest, and so most advanced, version of capitalist theory, and thus the basic economic theory invoked to justify global capitalism. It recommends free markets with a minimum of government regulation in the form of tax or control. Such deregulation tends to increase profit levels and facilitate speculation. Ideally, the state should be reduced to the smallest possible size and power. Privatisation of state utilities (health, education, transport and so on) is recommended by neo-liberalism, since it reduces state expenditure and the government's sphere of influence. In theory, privatisation cuts government expenditure, reduces tax levels, and gives opportunities for profit for private companies. The reduction of government expenditure pleases the richer citizens, who can buy both shares and all the services they need from schools, hospitals, transport systems etc. in the *private sector*. Neo-liberalism is, in its essence, a system designed to serve the rich.

Chris Harmer notes how the neo-liberal consensus rejects any alternative methods to regulate the system – for example, Keynesianism or state capitalism, let alone socialism. He continues:

But it is not only far reaching change which is ruled out. So are the mildest reforms – a minimum wage of more than about a third of the median [. . .], any attempt to protect jobs against the withering effects of recession. If workers push their demands too hard, then companies will simply pack up their bags and move elsewhere. If governments implement meaningful reforms, then new investments will simply flow to more profitable parts of the world.[62]

But the items that have been listed are, in fact, policies rather than theories. Neo-liberalism presents itself as a theory, but is in reality an inflexible set of prescriptions to protect wealth. It claims legitimacy from the writings of classical liberals, like Adam Smith, but actually follows policies which are very different from those which he recommended.

There is another discrepancy. Protectionism had emerged in the late 17th century to raise state revenue. It was believed that trade surpluses made a country richer, and protectionism helped this process.[63] Modern neo-liberalism recommends free trade, and that all countries stop protectionism. Yet, most of the major economic powers subsidise and protect their own industries. For example, Chomsky pointed out in 1997 that OECD figures showed US state funding for non-military research and development to be 'about one third of all civil research spending, as compared to 2 per cent state funding in Japan'.[64]

Third World countries, however, are not allowed to participate in such 'cheating'. For them, the playing field is deliberately not level at all. The whole economic system has the effect of maximising profit for rich countries, for companies operating in them and investors living in them, and minimising it for Third World countries.

This is the 'gap between doctrine and reality' that Chomsky is pointing to when he writes:

*If we take the trouble to distinguish **doctrine from reality** we find that the political and economic principles that have prevailed are remote from those that are proclaimed.*[65]

Writing in 1994, Chomsky notes how neo-liberal ideology is being used in a new class war. In a similar way, technology is being used for profit and power rather than humane purposes. The invoking of classical liberal economic theory serves as a cloak for the real aims of global capitalism (pursuit of enormous profits, enrichment of a small élite, further impoverishment of the poor). Technology is being integrated into this profit-oriented strategy in a way which creates 'a form of progress without people', but 'not as a consequence of the nature of technology or the pursuit of efficiency and cost-effectiveness'. In fact, as had happened in the early industrial revolution, the technology 'is designed to increase profit and power, ownership and managerial control at the expense of meaningful work, freedom, human life, and welfare'.[66]

The implementation of neo-liberal policies

often follows a standardised format called the Washington Consensus. In a way which is consistent with the principle of the gap between 'doctrine and reality', just mentioned, these policies tend to do the opposite of what they claim, ruining national economies rather than solving their economic problems, through the use of stringent structural adjustment programmes. Chomsky describes the basic rules of the Washington Consensus:

[L]*iberalize trade and finance, let markets set price (get prices right), end inflation (macro-economic stability), privatize. The government should get out of the way.*[67]

This structural adjustment programme will be discussed further in the next section.

Michel Chossudovsky, Professor of Economics at the University of Ottawa, describes the effects of price liberalisation:

Measures like price liberalisation have a dramatic effect on indebted countries, typically including low-growth, low-wage economies with high profits. They also tend to produce substantial rises in the domestic prices of fertiliser, farm inputs, equipment etc. which have an immediate impact in most areas of economic activity.[68]

The high profits are naturally accompanied by high returns for (normally foreign, especially US) investors.

Inevitably, as Chomsky makes clear, those who impose these rules have enormous power. They effectively have the fate of the economies of many nations under their control. Indeed, according to the international business press, as Chomsky points out, the bodies involved (e.g. the IMF (International Monetary Fund) and World Bank) effectively constitute the core of a '*de facto* world government' of a 'new imperial age'.[69]

Not so long ago, we used to believe that the last 'world empire' was the one named by Mrs Thatcher and President Reagan as the 'Evil Empire' of the Soviet Union. But there can be said to exist an empire to this day. Naturally, it is more discreet and more subtle. It avoids drawing too much attention to itself, but it is there all the same. At its centre, the Leader of the Free World, the USA. Working with it, America's allies, particularly Great Britain and the other members of NATO. Supporting it are the great international agencies like the World Bank, International Monetary Fund and World Trade Organisation. Unfortunately, as will be seen, there are good reasons for concern about the operations of these agencies.

One has to acknowledge the notable effectiveness of the empire's public relations and propaganda departments. Some readers may feel that these criticisms of the new world order are excessive or absurd, that everyone worldwide is happy and thriving, and that 'everything is for the best in the best of all possible worlds'.[70]

Review of Part I

The first part of this book dealt with globalisation, neo-liberalism and the new world order, mainly from the viewpoint of Noam Chomsky. Much of his work can be said to be about the ethics of power, and among his central concerns are freedom and creativity on the one hand, and democracy, justice and truth on the other. Chomsky has many targets in his sights, among them various US government policies, together with the inequality, poverty and other forms of damage imposed on people's lives by neo-liberal programmes. Yet underlying all these different concerns, it can be argued, is a sense of *rightness* and *order*, a recognition that something has gone wrong when 30 per cent of the world's population is unemployed, when the gap between rich and poor continues to grow steadily.

Far from being dazzled by the prospect of an exciting future of triumphant neo-liberalism (so efficient, so modern and so free), he foresees a possible world which has been taken over by, or on behalf of, super-rich élite groups, men who are working to turn the clock back more than two centuries, abolish workers' rights, and bring back the conditions of Blake's 'dark Satanic Mills'. Their plan, according to Chomsky, is to get rid of the welfare state for the workers, even though this would be at the risk of producing desperation, anxiety, hopelessness and fear, together with a continuing increase in inequality.[71]

This prospect of a worsening of life conditions for the majority seems all the more practicable in a world order in which the United States already controls a large part of global trade and business. With the aid of their prosperous Western allies, supported by subservient client states elsewhere; and buoyed up by the major banking and financial institutions (effectively capitalist international bodies), and, most important of all, by the mighty transnational corporations, the US has established a *de facto* world government which operates largely in secret, undermines and ignores legitimate elected bodies like the World Court and UNO (United Nations Organisation), and controls large parts of the world.[72]

(But note: At this particular point in world history, at the beginning of the third millennium, the USA is the dominant power, and acts accordingly. It uses its power to advance its own interests in the same way as great powers have always done since they first appeared. But this suggests that it is possible energetically to criticise aspects of current American government policy, yet at the same time to acknowledge the coherence and logic of some of them, particularly if one is prepared to take a long-term view on such matters as the North–South confrontation within the context of 500 years of European conquest of the world. In other words, the North has been attacking and attempting to conquer the South for five centuries now. In this context, US policy towards Latin America can be seen as part of an ongoing policy of self-interest.[73]

In a similar vein, Chomsky is not shy of mentioning the use of poison gas and air power by the British Foreign Secretary Winston Churchill, labelling Kurds and Afghans as uncivilised tribes and recalcitrant Arabs.[74] So too, the US is regularly attacked by Chomsky for particular acts and policies. But, as he himself points out, similar policies were followed in the past by its imperial predecessors, including Britain. World order, one could say, does not change in its essentials. However, the apparent force of this *it's-appalling-but-it's-normal* argument is upset by the exceptional might and military force of the US today. The extraordinary wealth and power of the only world superpower still in place today qualitatively alters the nature of the balance. Like inequality between people, gross imbalance of power risks leading to conflict and tyranny. The present level of US power is highly dangerous, particularly in a nation that has such a strong and largely unquestioned belief in its own virtuousness, and that often claims to be:

[L]*eader of the free world . . . champion of freedom . . . legitimate leader but actually more legitimate than indigenous leaders who did not meet the U.S. definition of freedom-loving behavior.*[75] Note ends)

To go back to our review of Part I, Chomsky showed in 1997 how the US government and the TNCs cooperated secretly in order to undermine democracy, and also to weaken and damage genuinely free markets. He wrote that the 'assaults on democracy and markets' were actually related to each other. Their roots lay in 'the power of corporate entities that are totalitarian in internal structure, increasingly interlinked and reliant on powerful states, and largely unaccountable to the public'.[76]

These unelected and unaccountable corporate entities produce extreme inequality, not only in Third World countries, but in rich ones as well, including the USA.[77]

The social policies now in use are turning the whole world into an expanded version of the Third World, a world in which inequality goes on expanding, 'with sectors of enormous wealth and privilege alongside of an increase in the proportion of those who will labor under all the hardships of life'. (Here Chomsky is quoting the American visionary statesman and fourth US president, James Madison (1751–1836).)[78]

Some commentators agree that the neo-liberal policy of deregulation has increased inequality.[79] Thus, the American economists Jeff Faux and Larry Mishel noted recently that:

At the very least, the recent accumulation of wealth has been extraordinary; in 1996 the

United Nations Development Programme (UNDP) reported that the assets of the world's 358 billionaires exceeded the combined incomes of 45 per cent of the world's population.[80]

Restructuring of Debt

The process of restructuring is one of the most striking if not dramatic examples in the operation of economic globalisation. The general effect of the restructuring of debt as an assault on Third World countries, changing the rules of banking in such a way as to make it difficult or impossible for them to pay off their debts to the IMF and World Bank, has been disastrous. The restructuring of loans in the 1980s by the IMF and World Bank involved their re-negotiation, so that the debtor nations had to pay much more interest and often had to raise prices, cut services (schools, hospitals, road-building) and hand over control of their economies to Western agencies and investors. Chomsky refers to the restructuring process at a number of points in his writings, quoting Chossudovsky on the application to

Russia of what was essentially 'a carbon copy of the structural adjustment program imposed on debtor countries in the Third World' by the IMF and World Bank. The official aim of this programme was to stabilise the economy, but its effect in Russia was 'to increase consumer prices a hundredfold in one year, to reduce real earnings by over 80 per cent, and to wipe out billions of roubles of life-long savings'. As elsewhere, the programme adopted in the name of democracy turned out to be 'a coherent program of impoverishment of large sectors of the population'.[81]

Hobsbawm, in his discussion of globalisation and debt restructuring, describes the last years of the 20th century as a period in which 'supranational decision-making' would grow quickly. To an increasing degree, the Great Powers were taking over control of the whole Earth. This control already operated:

[T]*hrough the global bank-managers of the great international lending-agencies, representing the joint resources of the oligarchy of the richest powers, which also happened to include the most powerful ones. As the gap between rich and poor grew, the scope for exercising global power looked like increasing.*

At this point, the link between global power and inequality becomes clearer. Hobsbawm goes on to explain how, 'since the 1970s, the World Bank and the International Monetary Fund, politically backed by the USA', had pursued a policy which 'systematically favour[ed] free-market orthodoxy, private enterprise and global free trade'. These liberal policies suited the late 20th century US economy as well as they had suited the mid-19th century British one. But they did not necessarily suit the rest of the world.[82]

When the International Monetary Fund was set up in 1944, it was as part of a world economic system with noble ideals. It aimed:

to facilitate the expansion of balanced growth of international trade, and to contribute thereby to the promotion and maintenance of high levels of employment and real income of the productive resources of all members and to bring about stability in exchange rates.

(Article I, clause 2 of the *Purposes of the International Monetary Fund*)[83]

In the 1980s, the era of Mrs Thatcher (Prime Minister 1979–90) and President Reagan (1980–8), there was a marked trend in the rich industrial countries towards neo-liberal policies. Thus, there was much talk:

[A]*bout tax cuts, deregulation, freedom of the markets, reducing the role of government in the economy, monetarism and privatization.*

A new, tough, almost merciless philosophy began to take over:

The triumph of the ultra-conservatives, with their free-market, no-nonsense approach to the poor in their own countries, was hardly the harbinger of a sympathetic approach to dealing with the problems of the South.[84]

Development of the Debt Crisis

N.A. Adams, in *Worlds Apart* (1993), summarises the stages of development of the debt crisis:

i. In the 1970s, there was a five-fold increase in international debt (this represents a 19 per cent rise each year) for non-OPEC developing countries, caused by the increase in the price of oil, and by the resulting recession in industrial countries which led them to import less from the Third World;

ii. There was a doubling in the price of oil in 1979–80;

iii. A steep rise in interest rates occurred through the US monetarist anti-inflation policy. For an average middle-income developing country, this meant a tripling in interest rates (6.6 per cent in 1976 to 17.5 per cent by 1981).[85]

The resulting recession was caused by anti-inflation policies in the US and other countries.

At this point, Chomsky continues the story, describing what happened in Mexico. The debt crisis first hit Mexico in August 1982, when the country was unable to raise enough money to pay its debts. In 1996, Chomsky described its impact. The number of people below the poverty level increased at roughly the same rate (i.e. from 1 to 24) as that at which new Mexican billionaires (friends of the president who had been allowed to buy major state assets at a fraction of their value) had just appeared in the official Forbes list. Wages fell by about 50 per cent.

Part of the point of NAFTA (North Atlantic Free Trade Association) was to undermine the Mexican economy by opening it up to much cheaper imports from the U.S. The U.S. has an advanced state-subsidized economy, so therefore you can produce things very cheaply. The idea was to wipe out middle-level Mexican business, keep the multinationals.

In other words, as Chomsky sardonically put it:

Keep the monopolies. Keep the billionaires. Lower wages. That's good for U.S. corporations.[86]

Apart from increasing sales of US products to the

Third World, the policy of restructuring debt and impoverishing Third World countries had a number of other objectives. These included:

Teaching poor countries a lesson

It is hard to resist the conclusion that one of the chief purposes of the debt strategy as it actually evolved, and of the harsh conditionalities that were imposed, was to teach the developing countries a lesson, to put them in their place, to so frighten and weaken them and make them so obviously dependent on the favours and subject to the dictates of the industrial North, that it would be a long, long time before they would ever again have the effrontery to attempt to confront the North with demands for a restructuring of the international economic order.[87]

Increasing dividends for Western investors

Another aim of the debt strategy of the West was to develop opportunities for Western investors. This has been achieved by subordinating the economies of the Third World to the economies of Western countries, and reorganising them so as to yield the maximum profit by the West. This is described in detail in Chossudovsky's important study, *Globalisation of Poverty*, which contains a review of the harmful consequences of the economic reforms imposed on the Third World by Western financial institutions. Chomsky praises this book in an enthusiastic endorsement on its back cover:

Chossudovsky's [. . .] general analysis and pene-trating case studies show how these 'reforms' restore colonial patterns, bar national planning and meaningful democracy, and undermine pro-grams which benefit the general population, while establishing the framework for a world of growing inequality, with a large majority con-signed to suffering and despair in the interests of narrow sectors of privilege and power.[88]

Chomsky takes a similar line when he refers to:

[T]*he economic catastrophe that swept much of the Third World, affecting the richer countries too, ever since the wave of liberalization and a specific form of 'globalization' imposed in the interests of the powerful.*[89]

In this connection, Chomsky describes the G-15 meeting in Jamaica which followed the meeting of the powerful G-7 nations in February 1999, and was attended by, as he puts it, such 'unimportant places' as India, Mexico, Chile, Brazil, Argentina, Indonesia, Egypt, Nigeria, Venezuela and Jamaica. This meeting laid particular stress on the need, in Chomsky's words, 'to impose conditions on financial flows so that speculative capital would not destroy economies at will'. With the IMF in the background acting as the credit community's 'enforcer' (as the then US executive director of the IMF put it), creditors made large profits from apparently risky loans, the risks being safely guaranteed and borne primarily by Western taxpayers who provided free risk insurance.[90]

In other words, it was, in effect, a case of taxpayers financing banks by guaranteeing their loans . . .

After the debt crisis of the early 1980s, how-ever, things had changed considerably. The IMF and World Bank were now carrying out pro-grammes of 'macro-economic stabilisation' and 'structural adjustment' on developing countries who needed to re-negotiate their external debt. Many of these countries were among those who had earlier borrowed large amounts of oil money when the interest rates were low, and had then got caught out and fallen into serious debt when the interest rates on loans had been raised. Many Third World countries were caught in this way, and the 'economic medicine' of the World Bank and IMF was applied to them.

The result of these adjustments has been to impoverish hundreds of millions of people, often over long periods of time. Thus, the structural adjustment programmes contributed largely to destabilising national currencies and ruining the economies of developing countries.

Michel Chossudovsky lists in detail the effects of the structural adjustment programme in coun-tries all over the world. Here are some examples:

- Collapse of the internal purchasing power of economies (p. 33).
- Outbreak of famines: Zimbabwe and Southern Africa, 1982 (pp. 106–7); Rwanda, 1987–91 (p. 115); Vietnam, mid-1980s (p. 147).
- Closing of clinics and schools, normally under World Bank supervision, requiring privatisation of schools and medicine, in former Eastern Bloc countries and Africa (p. 54).
- General breakdown in curative and preventative care as a result of lack of medical equipment and supplies, poor working conditions and low pay of medical personnel (p. 70).[91]

Chossudovsky describes the impact of the changes imposed on Third World and Eastern European countries by the IMF and the World Bank in accordance with neo-liberal 'principles'. He shows in detail how neo-liberal economic practice has serious social effects. The IMF regularly imposes devaluation on affected countries.

Chossudovsky goes on to describe how the social impact of the devaluation sponsored by the IMF has proved brutal and immediate:

- The domestic prices of basic foods, essential drugs, fuel and public services increase overnight.
- While the devaluation invariably triggers inflation and the dollarisation of domestic prices (with the result that *local* prices go right up to *world* levels), the IMF obliges the government (as part of the economic package) to adopt a so-called anti-inflationary programme. The real cause of the inflation is, of course, the IMF measures themselves, including the devaluation. Once it is realised that their real purpose is to help the US export industry by damaging that of the Third World, the actual reason for 'anti-inflationary measures' reveals itself to be hostile, not helpful.
- As a result of measures like these, for example, the devaluation of the Central and West African (CFA) franc which was imposed by the IMF and French Treasury in 1994 reduced, overnight, the real value of wages and government expenditure in hard currency by 50 per cent, and also redirected huge amounts of state revenues towards 'debt-servicing'.

The wretched saga of 'restructuring of Third World debt' provides another fairy story of global finance, or, as Chomsky puts it, another tale of theory and reality. Can one not speak here of 'wickedness and untruth'? It is like other tales of globalisation and the new world order: there is a gap between the claims and the facts. It was claimed that the restructuring, like the IMF at its formation, was there to help countries reorganise their economies, pay off their debt and move into surplus. In fact, it does the reverse. The policies purport to help the indebted countries to solve their debt problems, but actually drive them further into debt, and sometimes hand their economies over to foreign investors and TNCs. As part of the conditions imposed on loans, the debtor countries are often obliged to undermine their own industries and buy cheap, mass-produced goods from America. And all this to promote the very free trade that America will not practise itself. Whether it is a case of imposing free trade on poor countries (while rich ones continue to subsidise their industries), or a case of 'helping' poor countries by increasing their debt or undermining their industries, global capitalism always wins.

Thus it is no exaggeration to state that the debt restructuring programme has seriously damaged the very Third World countries it pretended to help:

- The newly negotiated loans actually increase the level of debt.
- Trade liberalisation makes the balance of payments worse by replacing domestic production with increased imports.
- With the formation of the World Trade Organisation, a greater part of the bill is now made up of services, such as intellectual property rights. The import bill of developing countries grows without there being a corresponding increase in the export of produced commodities.
- The IMF structural adjustment programme fails to promote growth in debtor nations. These must pay back their debt through exports before they can concentrate on domestic growth.

By an irony of fate, there is a final blow directed *against* the West by the technical efficiencies of globalisation. Developments in IT have made it easier for Western factories to use Third World labour to replace the workforce in advanced capitalist countries. Increasingly, work flies to where labour is cheapest. The prospects for workers in the West are already under threat. In California, for example, factory owners moved car plants across the Rio Grande into Mexico where production costs are only a quarter of those in the US.[92]

The Future

What, if anything, does Chomsky predict for the world under globalisation? In fact, he encourages neither optimism nor pessimism. He recognises the scale of the injustice and inequality that economic globalisation and US government policy cause. He is careful to avoid exaggeration, but does not underestimate the strength of the empire. However, to an important degree he is a humanist – a believer in people, in the value of work and in organising for political action. Challenging illegitimate claims to authority is still necessary. *La lutte continue*. The struggle goes on . . .

Faced with the daunting scale of global unemployment, with the nihilism of current devotion to the values of privilege, ambition and success, with the mercilessness of an economic order that cares for little else but profit, Chomsky presents us all with a simple choice:

Either – we acquiesce in global injustice and tyranny;

Or – we join in the struggle for justice, democracy and freedom.

How far can this go? Will it really be possible to construct an international society on something like the Third World model, with islands of great privilege in a sea of misery – fairly large islands, in the richer countries – and with controls of a totalitarian nature within democratic forms that increasingly become a façade? Or will popular resistance, which must itself become internationalized to succeed, be able to dismantle these evolving structures of violence and domination, and carry forth the centuries-old expansion of freedom, justice and democracy that is now being aborted, even reversed? These are the large questions for the future.[93]

Notes

1. *New York Times*, quoted in Noam Chomsky, *Terrorizing the neighbourhood – American foreign relations in the post-Cold War era*, Stirling, Scotland: AK Press, 1991, p. 5.

2. Comment from reader, Richard Hoffner, in letter about Kathleen Hendrix's interview article on Chomsky in *Los Angeles Times*, 2 March 1988.

3. Charles Darwin, *The Descent of Man, and Selection in Relation to Sex*, Princeton, NJ: Princeton University Press, 1981, Vol. 1, p. 166.

4. Chomsky, *World Orders, Old and New* (1994), London: Pluto Press, 1997, p. 43.

5. Garry Wills, 'Bully of the Free World', Washington: *Foreign Affairs*, Vol. 78, No. 2, March/April 1999, pp. 50–9.

6. Leading article, 'Europe must stand up to America's bullying tactics', London: *The Independent*, 5 March 1999, p. 3.

7. Chomsky, *Language and Politics* (1988), C.P. Otero (ed.), Montreal: Black Rose Books, 1999, p. 765.

8. James McGilvray, *Chomsky – language, mind and politics*, Cambridge, England: Polity Press, 1999, p. 178.

9. Ibid., pp. 178–9. (Statement by Chomsky.)

10. Note by editor, C.P. Otero, in Chomsky, *Language and Politics* (1988), 1999, p. 33.

11. Ibid., p. 34.

12. Ibid., p. 25.

13. Ibid., pp. 23–7.

14. Ibid., p. 774.

15. John Maher and Judy Groves, *Introducing Chomsky*, Cambridge, England: Icon Books, 1999, p. 120.

16. Chomsky, *Language and Politics* (1988), 1999, p. 260.

17. Ibid., p. 261.

18. Chomsky, *Radical Priorities* (1984), C.P. Otero (ed.), Montreal: Black Rose Books, 1995, p. 47.

19. Chomsky, *Language and Politics* (1988), 1999, p. 318.

20. McGilvray, *Chomsky – language, mind and politics*, 1999, p. 2.

21. Chomsky, *Language and Politics* (1988), 1999, p. 469.

22. Chomsky, *Chronicles of Dissent – interviews with David Barsamian*, Monroe, Maine: Common Courage Press, 1992, pp. xiii–xiv.

23. Chomsky, *Radical Priorities*, 1995, p. 44.

24. Chomsky, *Year 501 – the conquest continues*, London: Verso, 1993, pp. 141–274.

25. Chomsky, *Keeping the Rabble in Line – interviews with David Barsamian*, Edinburgh: AK Press, 1994, pp. 114–15.

26. Chomsky, *Class Warfare – interviews with David Barsamian*, London: Pluto Press, 1996, p. 34.

27. Ibid., pp. 22–5.

28. Chomsky, *Democracy in a Neoliberal Order: Doctrines and Reality*, University of Cape Town, 1997, e.g. p. 16.

29. Chomsky, *Powers and Prospects – Reflections on Human Nature and the Social Order*, London: Pluto Press, 1996, pp. 55–6.

30. TV programme, 'Noam Chomsky et les Médias', broadcast on French TV station Planète, May 2000.

31. Eric Hobsbawm, *Age of Extremes – the Short Twentieth Century* (1994), London: Abacus, 1999, p. 5.

32. Graham Evans and Jeffrey Newnham, *The Penguin Dictionary of International Relations*, Harmondsworth: Penguin, 1998, p. 201.

33. David Held, Anthony McGrew, David Goldblatt and Jonathan Perraton, *Global Transformations – politics, economics and culture*, Cambridge, England: Polity Press, 1999, p. 16.

34. Elaine Bernard, *A Short Guide to the WTO, the Millennium Round and the Rumble in Seattle*, ZNet Commentary, 24 November 1999. http://www.zmag.org

35. Held, et al., *Global Transformations*, 1999, p. 216.

36. Eric Hobsbawm, *The New Century*, London: Little, Brown and Company, 2000, p. 69.

37. James Paul Gee, Lynda Hull and Colin Lankshear, *The New Work Order – behind the language of the new capitalism*, St Leonards, Australia: Allen and Unwin, 1996, pp. 25–35.

NOTES

38. Chomsky, *Class Warfare*, 1996, p. 16.

39. Elizabeth Fones-Wolf, *Selling Free Enterprise*, University of Illinois Press, date not known. Quoted in Chomsky, *Class Warfare*, 1996, p. 17.

40. Pedro Agustín Díaz Arenas, *Relaciones Internacionales de Dominación*, Bogotá: Universidad Nacional de Colombia, 1998, p. 23.

41. Will Hutton and Anthony Giddens (eds), *On the Edge – Living with Global Capitalism*, London: Jonathan Cape, 2000, p. 12.

42. Chomsky, *For Reasons of State*, New York: Pantheon, 1973, pp. 403–4.

43. Held, et al., *Global Transformations*, 1999, pp. 1–10.

44. Jason Bennetto, Crime Correspondent, 'Police plan cyber force to tackle crime on the Internet', London: *The Independent*, 26 October 1999, p. 7.

45. Hutton and Giddens, *On the Edge*, 2000, pp. 213–23.

46. e.g. K. Ohmae, *The End of the Nation State*, New York: Free Press, 1995.

47. Paul Hirst and Graham Thompson, *Globalization in Question: the International Economy and the Possibilities of Governance*, Cambridge: Polity Press, 1996.

48. Held, et al., *Global Transformations*, 1999, pp. 7–9.

49. Hutton and Giddens, *On the Edge*, 2000, pp. 46–7.

50. cf. Hutton and Giddens, ibid., p. 12.

51. David Brown, *Cybertrends – chaos, power and*

accountability in the information age, London: Viking, 1997, p. 107.

52. Ibid., p. 103.

53. Robert Beynon (ed.), *The Icon Critical Dictionary of Global Economics*, Cambridge, England: Icon Books, 1999, p. xi.

54. President Clinton, 'Globalisation – America's final frontier', last 'state of the Union' message, London: *The Independent Review*, 31 January 2000, p. 4.

55. cf. Jeff Faux and Larry Mishel, 'Inequality and the Global Economy', in Hutton and Giddens, *On the Edge*, 2000, pp. 93–111.

56. Quoted in Diana Coyle, 'Head of WTO hits out at Seattle rioters in defence of free trade', London: *The Independent,* 17 June 2000, p. 19.

57. Chomsky, personal communication, 10 February 2000.

58. William Finnegan, *Cold New World – growing up in a harder country*, London: Picador, 1999, p. xiii.

59. Hobsbawm, *The New Century*, 2000, p. 164.

60. Chomsky, *Profit over People – Neoliberalism and the Global Order*, New York: Seven Stories Press, 1999, p. 20.

61. Chomsky, *Class Warfare*, 1996, p. 20.

62. Chris Harmer, 'Globalisation: a critique of a new orthodoxy', London: *International Socialist*, No. 73, 1996, pp. 3–4.

63. Held, et al., *Global Transformations*, 1999, p. 154.

64. Chomsky, *World Orders, Old and New* (1994), 1997, p. 107.

65. Chomsky, *Democracy in a Neoliberal Order*, 1997, p. 33. Also published in Chomsky, *Profit over People*, 1999, pp. 91–118.

66. Chomsky, *World Orders, Old and New* (1994), 1997, p. 186.

67. Chomsky, *Profit over People*, 1999, p. 20.

68. Michel Chossudovsky, *The Globalisation of Poverty – impacts of IMF and World Bank Reforms*, London: Zed Books, 1997, p. 61.

69. Chomsky, *Profit over People*, 1999, p. 20.

70. Reference to Pangloss, the eternal optimist in Voltaire's *Candide* (1759). Pangloss is a parody of the German philosopher G. W. Leibniz (1646–1716).

71. Chomsky, *Class Warfare*, 1996, pp. 9–10.

72. cf. Chomsky, *The New Military Humanism – Lessons from Kosovo*, London: Pluto Press, 1999, pp. 148–9.

73. cf. Chomsky, *World Orders, Old and New* (1994), 1997, pp. 43–4.

74. Chomsky, *Necessary Illusions – thought control in democratic societies*, London: Pluto Press, 1989, p. 182; *Chronicles of Dissent*, Stirling, Scotland: AK Press, 1992, p. 308; *Year 501 – the contest continues*, 1993, p. 23; *The New Military Humanism*, 1999, p. 62.

75. Garry Wills, 'Bully of the Free World', in *Foreign Affairs*, 1999, pp. 50–9.

76. Chomsky, *Democracy in a Neoliberal Order*, 1997, p. 2.

77. William Finnegan, *Cold New World*, 1999, passim.

78. Chomsky, *Democracy in a Neoliberal Order*, 1997, p. 2.

79. e.g. David Brown, *Cybertrends*, 1997, pp. 107–10.

80. Faux and Mishel, 'Inequality and the Global Economy', in Hutton and Giddens, *On the Edge*, 2000, p. 93.

81. Chomsky, *World Orders, Old and New* (1994), 1997, p. 152.

82. Hobsbawm, *Age of Extremes* (1994), 1999, p. 578.

83. Quoted in Robert Myers, *The Political Morality of the International Monetary Fund – Ethics and Foreign Policy*, Oxford: Transaction Books, Vol. 3, 1987, pp. 1–2.

84. Nassau A. Adams, *Worlds Apart: the North–South Divide and the International System*, London: Zed Books, 1993, p. 150.

85. Ibid., p. 150.

86. Chomsky, *Class Warfare*, 1996, p. 41.

87. Adams, *Worlds Apart*, 1993, p. 170.

88. Chomsky, comment on back cover of Chossudovsky, *The Globalisation of Poverty*, 1997.

89. Chomsky, *The New Military Humanism*, 1999, p. 148.

90. Ibid., pp. 148–9.

91. Chossudovsky, *The Globalisation of Poverty*, 1997, passim.

92. Chomsky, *World Orders, Old and New* (1994), 1997, pp. 162–3.

93. Ibid., p. 188.

Further Reading

About globalisation and the new world order

Robert Beynon (ed.), *The Icon Critical Dictionary of Global Economics*, Cambridge, England: Icon Books, 1999.

Michel Chossudovsky, *The Globalisation of Poverty – impacts of IMF and World Bank Reforms*, London: Zed Books, 1997.

James Paul Gee, Lynda Hull and Colin Lankshear, *The New Work Order – behind the language of the new capitalism*, St Leonards, Australia: Allen and Unwin, 1996.

John Gray, *False Dawns: The Delusions of Global Capitalism*, London: Granta Books, 1998.

David Held, Anthony McGrew, David Goldblatt and Jonathan Perraton, *Global Transformations – politics, economics and culture*, Cambridge, England: Polity Press, 1999.

Edward S. Herman and Robert W. McChesney, *The Global Media – the new missionaries of corporate capitalism*, London: Cassell, 1997.

Eric Hobsbawm, *The New Century*, London: Little Brown and Company, 2000.

Will Hutton and Anthony Giddens (eds), *On the Edge – Living with Global Capitalism*, London: Jonathan Cape, 2000.

George Soros, *The Crisis of Global Capitalism: Open*

Society Endangered, New York: BBS/Public Affairs, 1998.

About Chomsky
John Maher and Judy Groves, *Introducing Chomsky*, Cambridge, England: Icon Books, 1999.

James McGilvray, *Chomsky – language, mind and politics*, Cambridge, England: Polity Press, 1999.

James Peck, *The Chomsky Reader*, New York: Pantheon Books, 1987.

By Chomsky
Noam Chomsky, *Language and Politics* (1988), C.P. Otero (ed.), Montreal: Black Rose Books, 1999.

Noam Chomsky, *Radical Priorities* (1981), C.P. Otero (ed.), Montreal: Black Rose Books, second revised edition, 1995.

Noam Chomsky, *World Orders, Old and New* (1994), London: Pluto Press, 1997. **Strongly recommended.**

Noam Chomsky, *Profit over People – Neoliberalism and the Global Order*, New York: Seven Stories Press, 1999.

Noam Chomsky, *The New Military Humanism – Lessons from Kosovo*, London: Pluto Press, 1999.

Key Ideas

The ideas here are first given in outline, then presented in the form of quotations from Chomsky. The topics include the role of the US in the global economy, neo-liberal reforms in Russia, unemployment, and poverty.

1. The US government and major TNCs basically run the world to maximise American profits.

The 'principal architects' of the neoliberal 'Washington consensus' are the masters of the private economy, mainly huge corporations that control much of the international economy and have the means to dominate policy formation as well as the structuring of thought and opinion. The United States has a special role in the system for obvious reasons . . . the diplomatic historian Gerald Haines said 'Following World War II the United States assumed, out of self-interest, responsibility for the welfare of the world capitalist system'.

The United States had been the world's major economy long before World War II, and during the war it prospered while its rivals were severely weakened. . . . By the war's end, the United States had half of the world's wealth and a position of power without historical precedent. Naturally, the principal architects of policy intended to

use this power to design a global system in their interests.
(*Profit over People*, 1999, p. 20)

2. The profit-driven global system seems indifferent to the problem of global unemployment.

The International Labor Office estimates that about 30 per cent of the world's labor force was unemployed in January 1994.

Vast unemployment exists alongside of huge demands for labour. Wherever one looks, there is work to be done of great social and human value, and there are plenty of people eager to do that work. But the economic system cannot bring together needed work and the idle hands of suffering people. Its concept of economic health is geared to the demands of profit, not the needs of the people.
(*World Orders, Old and New*, 1997, p. 188)

3. The global system used neo-liberal 'reforms' to bring Russia to its knees.

In Russia alone, a UNICEF enquiry in 1993 estimated that half a million extra deaths a year result from the neoliberal 'reforms', which it generally supports. Russia's social policy chief recently estimated that 25 per cent of the population has fallen below subsistence levels, while the new rulers have gained enormous wealth, again the familiar pattern of Western dependencies.

(*Profit over People*, 1999, p. 24)

4. Prospects are dim for ordinary people all over the world through the possible erosion of the social contract.

[Global policy makers] *feel they can now roll back and unravel the entire social contract which developed through large-scale popular struggle over a century and a half, which did sort of soften the edges of predatory private tyranny, and often softened them a lot. In Germany, for example, workers have fairly reasonable conditions. So that has to be rolled back, and we have to go back to the days when we had wage slavery, as it was called by working people in the nineteenth century. No rights. The only rights you get are the rights you earn on the labor market. If your children can't make enough money to survive, they starve. Your choices are the workhouse prison, the labor market, whatever you can get there.*

(*Class Warfare*, 1996, p. 18)

5. US protectionism provides an excellent health service for the rich, but nobody else.

[The makers of global policy] *always wanted a very powerful state which intervenes massively, but it's a welfare state for the rich. That's the way the U.S. was founded. In fact, the U.S. pioneered that development. It's been the most protectionist of all the industrial societies. The U.S. has always been a pioneer and a bastion of protectionism, which is why it's a rich, powerful country . . .*

. . . For poor people and working people, they have to be subjected to market discipline. That part is true. But the other side, which is less said, is that rich people are going to have a nanny state protecting and subsidizing them, and a powerful one.

(*Class Warfare*, 1996, p. 18)

Acknowledgement

Particular thanks are due to Professor Noam Chomsky for all his help. Not only did he provide the base material which is summarised in this book, but he also gave valuable guidance and information. Finally, he shows us what it is to work unstintingly to build a juster world.